Read Along Rhymes

These rhyming stories help to make early reading an exciting, enjoyable shared experience for children, parents and teachers. They are designed to be read by adult and child together, or by children in pairs. The 'join-in' or 'read along' text is contained in speech bubbles, giving children an active role in the story-telling. The pictures and speech bubbles together give the outline of the story – the full story is told in the verse below. *Read Along Rhymes* can be used in conjunction with any reading programme.

The stories can be used flexibly, as perfect 'take-home books', linking home and school. They can also be used by teachers as part of their language programme, matching a book to a child, and developing the content within each book.

Read Along Stories

If you've enjoyed *Read Along Rhymes* you will be sure to get a lot of fun out of *Read Along Stories* (25 titles).

1	The Hungry Snake	14	The Little Indian
2	Fresh Fish on Friday	15	The Strange Umbrella
3	The Mischievous Monkey	16	The Envious Elephant
4	Gilbert the Goat	17	An Orange for the Baby
5	Hen Looks for a House	18	The Magic Vase
6	The Clever Worm	19	The Two Wizards
7	The Robber Rat	20	The King who Couldn't Kick
8	Dirty Dan	21	The Queen who Wouldn't be Quiet
9	Mr Tubb's Tap	22	Snakes and Ladders
10	The Witch's Ball	23	Yawn Yawn Yawn
11	Ant's Apple	24	A Jumper for Grumper
12	Nails for Newt	25	Peter's Pink Panda
13	Cat's Cake		

Suggestions to parents

It's a good idea to try and find a quiet place to sit together, away from distractions. First look through the pictures together, stop and talk about what's happening in the story: what's in the pictures, how the characters are feeling, what's going to happen next, and so on. You can have fun with the repetitions, the exclamations and the rollicking rhythms of the verse.

Edwina the Explorer

Edwina loved adventure,
She wanted to explore.
'I'm off to see the world,' she said,
'I'll write from Ecuador.'

First she climbed Mount Everest.
'It's jolly cold up here.
I haven't seen a Yeti yet.
Perhaps there's one round here?'

'This blizzard's really awful,
I wish the snow would stop.
Whoops! Just missed an avalanche.
At last I've reached the top.'

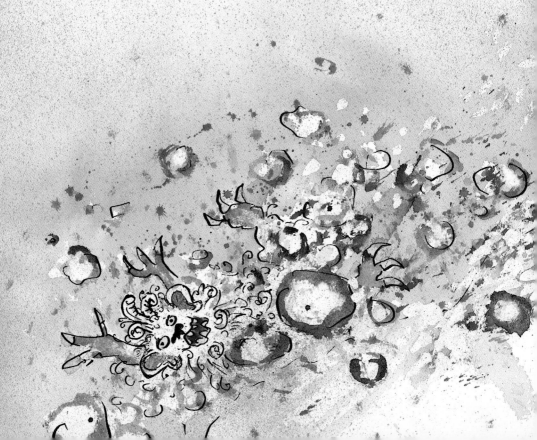

Next she sailed to Trinidad
To look for Spanish gold.
She found an ancient galleon.
'Is there treasure in the hold?'

She saw the rusty cannons,
She swam around the wreck.
At last she found the treasure–
It was down below the deck.

She paddled down the Amazon
In a dugout log canoe.
She saw some fierce piranhas
And an anaconda too.

She wanted to explore the bank.
The forest dripped with rain.
She found too many hungry ants
And jumped back in again.

She travelled to the desert
And joined a camel train.
They crossed the great Sahara.
For weeks there was no rain.

The water bags were empty.
'This heat is killing me.'
Then someone saw a water-hole.
'At last a cup of tea!'

Edwina came back home again
To see her mum and dad.
She told them her adventures
And all the fun she'd had.

She said goodnight and went upstairs.
She'd just got into bed
When suddenly there was a crash –
The shelf fell on her head!

Edwina sat in hospital.
'I'm off to see Peru!
It isn't very safe at home,
My head is black and blue!'

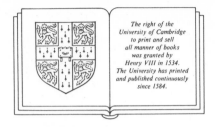

Published by the Press Syndicate of the University of Cambridge
The Pitt Building, Trumpington Street, Cambridge CB2 1RP
32 East 57th Street, New York, NY 10022, USA
10 Stamford Road, Oakleigh, Melbourne 3166, Australia

First Published 1989

Printed in Hong Kong by Wing King Tong

British Library cataloguing in publication data
Potter, Tessa
  Edwina the explorer
  1. English language. Readers – For children
  I. Title II. Vyvyan-Jones, Marc III. Series
  428.6

ISBN 0 521 35494 3 hard covers
ISBN 0 521 35759 4 paperback

DS